PIANO · VOCAL · GUITAR

Disney · PIXAR

Cars 3

ISBN 978-1-5400-0044-6

HAL•LEONARD®

7777 W. BLUEMOUND RD. P.O. BOX 13819 MILWAUKEE, WI 53213

Visit Hal Leonard Online at
www.halleonard.com

KINGS HIGHWAY

Words and Music by
TOM PETTY

Moderate Rock

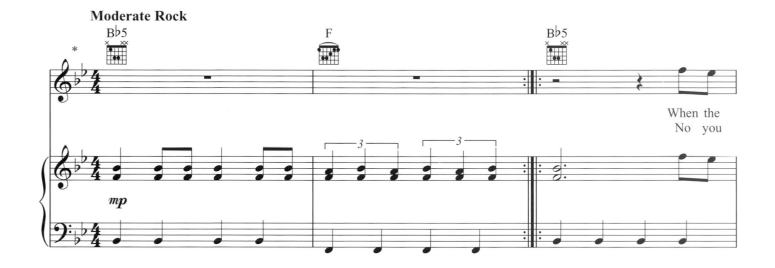

When the
No you

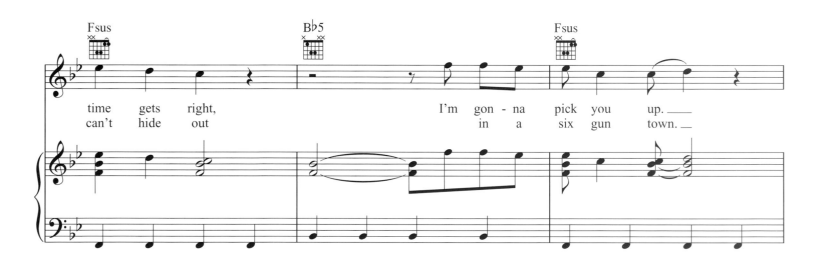

time gets right,
can't hide out

I'm gon - na   pick you   up. ___
in a   six gun   town. ___

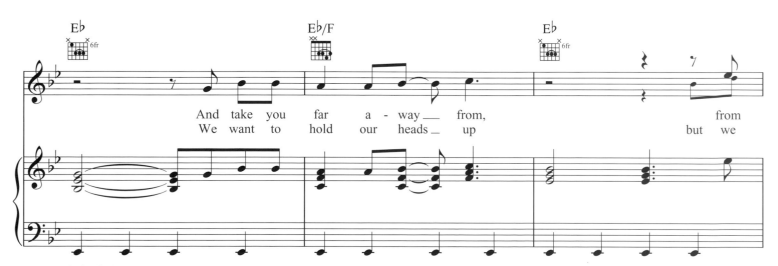

And take you   far a - way ___ from,
We want to   hold   our heads ___ up

from
but we

Recorded a half step higher.

for- tune comes ___ our way ___ and we ride ___ down the Kings ___ High - way, ___

yeah. ___

RUN THAT RACE

Words and Music by
DAN AUERBACH

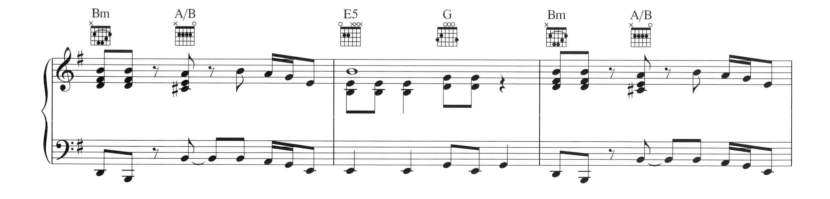

still there's love that I know. *Instrumental solo*

TRUCKAROO

Music by BRAD PAISLEY

Fast Country beat

GLORY DAYS

Words and Music by
BRUCE SPRINGSTEEN

Strong Shuffle groove

Oh, ___ I had a friend, ___ was a big base - ball ___ play-er back ___ in ___ high school. ___ He could throw that speed- ball right _____ by ya, make you look _____ like a fool.

(Woo.) _   (Woo.) _   *Solo ends*

I think I'm go-ing down to the well __ to - night. ___ I'm gon-na drink till I

get my fill. _____ And I hope when I get

old, I don't sit a-round talk-ing 'bout it; but I know I

RIDE

Words and Music by ZSUZSANNA WARD,
DAVE BASSETT and EVAN BOGART

FREEWAY OF LOVE

Words and Music by NARADA MICHAEL WALDEN
and JEFFREY COHEN

I knew you'd be a vi-sion in white. ___ How'd ___ you get your pants so tight? ___ Don't ___ know what you're do-in', but you must be liv-in' right. We

free - way of ___ love ___ in my pink Ca - dil - lac. ___

N.C.

We're _

___ rid - in' on the free - way of ___ love; wind's a - gainst our back. _

F

Repeat and Fade

Optional Ending

DRIVE MY CAR

Words and Music by JOHN LENNON
and PAUL McCARTNEY

Moderately, with a beat

Asked a girl what she want-ed to be. ___ She said, "Ba - by,
I told the girl that my pros-pects were good, ___ and she said, "Ba - by, it's
I told that girl I could start right a - way, ___ and she said, "Lis-ten, babe, I got

can't you see? ___ I wan-na be fa-mous, a star of the screen, ___ but
un - der - stood. ___ Work-ing for pea-nuts is all ver - y fine, ___ but
some-thing to say. I got no car and it's break-ing my heart, ___ but

you can do some-thing in be - tween: ___
I can show you a bet - ter time: ___
I found a driv - er, and that's a start: ___

Ba - by, you can drive my car, ___

To Coda